LARRY BURKETT

MAJOR PURCHASES

MOODY PRESS
CHICAGO

© 1991 by
CHRISTIAN FINANCIAL CONCEPTS

Compiled from material originally published by Christian Financial Concepts, Inc.

ISBN: 0-8024-2601-8

1 2 3 4 5 6 Printing/VP/Year 95 94 93 92 91

Printed in the United States of America

About the Author

Larry Burkett is committed to teaching God's people His principles for managing money. Unfortunately, money management is one area often neglected by Christians, and it is a major cause of conflict and disruption in both business and family life.

For more than two decades Larry has counseled and taught God's principles for finance across the country. As director of Christian Financial Concepts, Larry has counseled, conducted seminars, and written numerous books on the subject of maintaining control of the budget. In additon he is heard on more than 1000 radio outlets worldwide.

Major Purchases

How "Things" Demand Attention

Before we discuss major purchases—items such as a home, automobiles, or major appliances—we need to review the general impact of material possessions on our lives. Financial decisions based upon scriptural principles related to such large items as a home or car may greatly affect our financial future. Yet our attitude toward "things" as related to our relationship to God is even more important.

The affluence of the American way of life is a mixed blessing. On the positive side, our prosperity has made life much easier and has freed up a great deal of money to spread God's Word. But on the negative side, prosperity requires a great deal of our time and attention. In fact, the urgency of our materialistic lifestyles becomes a tyranny that demands most of our energies. It would seem that the labor cycle since the industrial revolution is reversing itself. Industrialization provided a higher standard of living with a shorter work week. In the early 1900s it took every family member working sixty hours per week just to make ends meet. By the mid-twentieth century, the average work week was forty-eight hours, and in most families the husband was the primary wage earner. Now in more than 70 percent of American families two incomes are again necessary to support the family's lifestyle.

Concern About the Future

Only a couple of decades ago the American dream was a good job, a comfortable home, and a nice car. Today it has become guaranteed employment, retirement plans, a home, two cars, a summer cottage, and college educations for all the kids. The possession of "things" has become the scorecard to determine "success." The pressure to provide the luxuries that have now become commonplace causes many Christian families to encumber themselves with debts that eventually destroy marriages. It's not surprising that many couples look back on their early years of marriage as the best, even though materially they were the leanest. Their lives were usually focused on the day-to-day events then, and, before mass media advertising, most of us didn't even know what we were missing. It seems clear that the Lord would have all of us focus more on today and less on the uncertainty of the future. "Therefore do not be anxious for tomorrow; for tomorrow will care for itself. Each day has enough trouble of its own" (Matthew 6:34).

MAKING LIFE EASIER

The primary purpose of material things is to make our lives easier and more comfortable. But it's amazing how complicated they can become. A family wants to spend a relaxing vacation in the mountains or at the beach, so they buy a summer cottage in that area. Then they find they must spend most of their free time keeping it repaired or protecting it from vandals. Often the experience is so bad that they end up loathing the very thing they thought would make life easier. Many times Christians get trapped into operating by the world's wisdom rather than God's.

Major Purchases

The world says, "Whatever you see and desire, acquire." God's Word says, "But seek for His kingdom, and these things shall be added to you" (Luke 12:31).

THE REAL PURPOSE OF THINGS

A survey of the scriptural warnings about riches and their dangers might seem to suggest that we should avoid all luxuries. That simply is not true. God does not prohibit us from enjoying the benefits of this world (after all, they are His). Rather, we are admonished not to get entangled in them to the point that we are no longer able to fulfill our primary purpose—serving God. "No soldier in active service entangles himself in the affairs of everyday life, so that he may please the one who enlisted him as a soldier" (2 Timothy 2:4). Unfortunately, today that is exactly what most Christians do. Individual ownership is a biblical principle, but carried to the extreme it becomes greed.

The real purpose of our resources is to free us to do more for Christ, not less. When the pursuit of things becomes our focus in life, there can be no doubt about whom we serve. "No one can serve two masters; for either he will hate the one and love the other, or he will hold to one and despise the other. You cannot serve God and mammon" (Matthew 6:24). The danger is more than just becoming enmeshed in this world. It is that we will lose our first love and our only source of peace.

"Do not love the world, nor the things in the world. If anyone loves the world, the love of the Father is not in him" (1 John 2:15). Consistently God's Word teaches that focusing on material things is the greatest danger we face. What makes it seem so normal today is that virtually everyone in America is doing it. Our great abundance has made us less— not more—content.

FIVE DANGERS OF THINGS

ADJUSTING TO A LIFE
OF INDULGENCE AS NORMAL

It is amazing that in less than fifty years we have grown to accept guaranteed salaries, insurance for every contingency, retirement benefits, and two-car families as normal. When the economy can't supply those things quickly enough, we simply mortgage our future generations to pay for them. The fruits of that selfishness are short-lived because eventually we borrow more than can ever be repaid. But the real reason this debt-funded economy always fails is that it violates basic biblical principles. "A faithful man will abound with blessing, but he who makes haste to be rich will not go unpunished" (Proverbs 28:20).

FOCUSING ON WORLDLY SUCCESS

For people who have committed themselves to an eternity with God, it's amazing how worldly our value system has become. We award positions of authority in our churches and organizations most often on the basis of material success rather than spiritual maturity. Obviously many Christians are materially and spiritually mature, but when we esteem people on the basis of material success, we begin to equate riches with spirituality. Thus, those who are not materially successful are deemed less spiritual. To be assured that God does not hold to the same value system, observe the apostles. "To this present hour we are both hungry and thirsty, and are poorly clothed, and are roughly treated, and are homeless" (1 Corinthians 4:11).

ULLING GOD'S DIRECTION

Nothing prohibits Christians from obeying God more than the tug of material comforts. Once we have adjusted to a lifestyle that includes many comforts, it is difficult to surrender them to serve God. Obviously God doesn't call everyone to leave his vocation and go into what is traditionally called "Christian work." God can and does use Christians everywhere. But in order to be used by God in any capacity, a Christian must be willing to serve God no matter what the cost. "I count all things to be loss in view of the surpassing value of knowing Christ Jesus my Lord, for whom I have suffered the loss of all things, and count them but rubbish in order that I may gain Christ" (Philippians 3:8).

Whenever someone asked Christ what would be expected of him as a follower, He always tested his or her willingness to surrender everything for God's sake. Without that attitude we can't even be trusted with material riches because we would spend them on our own indulgences or build larger barns to store them in.

But God's Word says, "And without faith it is impossible to please Him, for he who comes to God must believe that He is, and that He is a rewarder of those who seek Him" (Hebrews 11:6). We must believe that God wants to bless us, and until God individually convicts someone that His plan is otherwise, we are not to accept failure. Tribulation brings about proved character. Don't withdraw because of failure. Learn from it. Perseverance is lacking in Christianity today. Some Christians who fail get defeated and think that God has abandoned them. Some despair to the point of depression or suicide.

ADOPTING AN ATTITUDE OF SUPERIORITY

You would think that knowing everything belongs to God would make even the wealthiest among us humble. But it's sad what a little material success will do to our ego and pride. Few Christians can really handle success well. Some of the most devoted men of God have been sorely tested when they became known well enough to be a celebrity. Those who have been given responsibility in this life must be careful to exercise it with great caution, lest they give up their eternal rewards for temporary ones. "Do nothing from selfishness or empty conceit, but with humility of mind let each of you regard one another as more important than himself" (Philippians 2:3).

INDIFFERENCE TOWARD THE NEEDS OF OTHERS

A danger of material affluence is that we begin to think everybody has it. But that's simply not true. The vast majority of people in this world go to bed hungry and wake up hungry. They love their children as much as we do ours, and every day they die a little bit more because they cannot provide even the little food it takes to keep them alive. Let me assure you that most of them aren't lazy or evil—they are poor. They are the ones Christ describes in Matthew 25:45: "Then He will answer them, saying, 'Truly I say to you, to the extent that you did not do it to one of the least of these, you did not do it to Me.'"

Most often our indifference is passive. It isn't that Christians don't care (we do). It's just that we don't personally know any really poor people, and we're wary of the give-away plans of many ministries. But let me assure you, there are many really poor people and legitimate ministries who care for them individually. Giving to feed the poor and homeless is a command, not a request. This area seems to be the biggest lack in Christians today and is a direct result of our great affluence. It's unfortunate that the people in need are the most sensitive to the needs of others. (For further discussion on giving, see *Giving and Tithing* in this series.)

ESTABLISH A BALANCE

There must always be a balance in the area of material things. God does not have an identical plan for all of us, and what one family spends may be vastly different from another. The common measure for all of us is to achieve that balance between using our possessions and being controlled by them. To do this, a Christian must establish that he serves Christ first and all other considerations are secondary. That means that all of our actions should be heavily weighted to Christ's service first. Our giving should reflect this commitment, and a tithe should not be our goal but rather our minimum. Each increase in our income should increase our out-

reach before it "improves" our lifestyle. We should be known primarily
for our commitment to God's work
rather than for our display of material things.

Housing

The cost of buying or renting suitable housing for your family is perhaps the greatest expense you'll ever incur, so you must study your personal situation, research the possibilities, and pray for the Lord's guidance in order to make an educated decision about finding what's right for you.

CONSIDER THE VARIABLES

Before you decide whether to rent or buy a house, you must determine how much you can afford to spend for housing. If you are not actively living on a budget, you should make this your first step. *The Financial Planning Workbook* and *Personal Finances* (available through your local Christian bookstore) will help you set up a written financial plan.

Although your financial situation will be the major factor determining what type of housing you choose, other variables must also be considered. Prayerfully give these questions some thought:

1. Is your job secure enough to take on a mortgage? If not, consider renting instead of buying a house.
2. How long do you plan on staying in the area? If you know you will be staying in the community for an extended time—five to seven years at least—home ownership may be a good option.
3. What is the economy like in the area you are considering? Is the area growing substantially, and will the house appreciate? You don't want to be stuck with a house that you can't sell because of a poor economy.
4. What is the cost of living in the area? If it is high, it will definitely affect your budget and may change the amount you can afford for housing.

After answering these questions, take the amount you can spend for housing and determine if house payments, including taxes and insurance, would be equal to or less than rental payments for a similar house in the same area. If they would be, then buying a home may be a wise choice.

BIBLICAL PRINCIPLES TO CONSIDER

BORROWING

God doesn't prohibit borrowing, but He certainly does discourage it. In fact, every biblical reference to it is negative. Consider Proverbs 22:7, "The rich rules over the poor, and the borrower becomes the lender's slave." Home owners who lose their jobs and are unable to keep up with the payments find out firsthand what it's like to be in the position of a slave. Also, remember that borrowing is literally a vow to repay, and God requires that we keep our vows. "The wicked borrows and does not pay back" (Psalm 37:21). Keep these principles in mind when considering borrowing money to buy a house.

SURETY

Another biblical principle that affects you when you borrow money is "surety." Proverbs 17:18 says, "A man lacking sense pledges, and becomes surety in the presence of his neighbor." Surety is taking on an obligation to pay later without a certain way to pay. In a literal sense, surety means to deposit a pledge in either money, goods, or part payment for a greater obligation. When you sign surety for a debt, you pledge your future against that obligation. Thus, when you sign surety, you presume God's will. If there is no certain way to pay the debt, surety results. For example, if you buy a house and put up a 5 percent down payment and finance 95 percent, the real estate market needs to decrease only 5 percent for you to risk being caught in surety. But if you put 20 to 30 percent down on a house and finance 80 to 70 percent, your risk of being caught in surety is not as great. If you're going to borrow to buy, accumulate enough for a sizeable down payment.

The best way to avoid surety, however, is to make sure that any money you borrow is fully collateralized. Suppose you bought land that cost $10,000, and you put $1,000 down and borrowed $9,000. The terms of your contract should stipulate, "If I can't pay for this land, I give you the right to take the land back and keep all the money I've paid, but I'm released from all personal liabilities." A statement that releases you from personal liability for the loan is called an "exculpatory clause." Unfortunately, most institutions hold you personally responsible for mortgages and don't allow exculpatory clauses in their contracts. Surety is a biblical principle, not a law, but it will certainly come to haunt you when you can least afford it.

RENTING A HOUSE

If you have decided that renting a house is a better option for you at this time, there are several things to consider. First, decide what type of dwelling you want to rent. You can rent a house, apartment, town house, mobile home, or even a room or suite in someone else's house. The people in your church are often a good source of information about availability, location, and cost of rentals around the area.

TYPES OF LEASES

There are two main types of leases. One is a month-to-month lease, and the other is a lease for a specified amount of time—usually six months or one year. The month-to-month lease is great if you aren't sure how long you will be in the area or if you are waiting for a house to be finished. The problem with this type of lease is that the rent can be raised with simply a thirty-day notice. You can avoid this problem with a six-month or yearly lease. The rental price is renegotiated at the end of the lease term, and you can choose to stay and pay more or move out.

DEPOSITS

A security deposit is usually required when you sign a lease. This deposit can be retained by the owner if you damage the property while you are renting or if you have to move before your lease is up. A cleaning, pet, or key deposit may also be required. These are usually refunded when you turn in your keys and the owner inspects the property.

RENTER'S INSURANCE

The purpose of renter's insurance is threefold. It covers the value of your furniture and personal belongings and protects you from being sued by the owner's insurance company if there is damage to the property, such as grease fire or water damage. It also covers the liability if someone else is hurt on the property because of your or your children's negligence, i.e., someone falls or trips over a toy and is injured. Content and liability insurance usually costs about $100 to $150 a year and is well worth it, unless you can afford to replace all your belongings and have plenty of money on hand to cover exposed liabilities.

BUYING A HOUSE

If you've determined that purchasing a house fits into your budget and is in your best long-term interests, you can begin to look at the options available to you. You might consider these different types of dwellings: house, which includes building a new house or rebuilding a "fixer-upper," condominium, or mobile home.

HOUSE

First you will need to decide whether you want to purchase a new or used house. The advantages of building a new house are that you can design your house to fit your individual needs and locate it where you want it. The disadvantage of a new house is that, with few exceptions, those who build a new house end up spending more money than they planned. Changes made while the house is being built cost a lot of money, and it takes considerable time and mental effort to oversee the construction of a new house.

The advantages of buying a used house are that you know exactly what it is going to cost, and you can get more extras. Used houses usually come with curtains, curtain rods, towel racks, lights in the closets, light bulbs, an established lawn, shrubbery, and occasionally appliances. Make sure the contract states exactly which items will come with the house. The disadvantages of a used house are that any time a house has been lived in, it has some wear and tear. The older the house, the more things that will need repair. You should always check the heating and air conditioning, roof, hot water heater, and appliances to see if they are in working condition. You may choose to hire someone to do this for you. Then you can decide whether to purchase the house as is or back out of the deal.

THE FIXER-UPPER, OR
HANDY-MAN'S SPECIAL

Another alternative is a fixer-upper. This type of a house can be purchased at a relatively lower cost than other previously owned houses. But you will need to take into consideration the additional funds required beyond normal housing allocation for repairs. Be sure to check the house thoroughly, including foundation, plumbing, and wiring, so you know exactly what is wrong with the house before you buy it. If you have the skills and don't mind doing the repairs, you can make a nice profit when you sell it.

CONDOMINIUM

Another option is a condominium. You need to be aware of the additional costs beyond the purchase price, such as maintenance fees and club fees, if you wish to use the amenities available in a private community. Be aware that the maintenance fees are subject to change each year, and you have no control over them. This is not a bad option, especially if you don't want to bother with yard work.

MOBILE HOME

Although some people won't consider living in manufactured housing because of stereotypes about this type of housing, many couples purchase mobile homes and think they are great. It gives them better housing than they could afford otherwise and satisfies the needs of their families. This may be an option for older couples who are retiring and don't want to have to care for a large home.

The major disadvantage of manufactured housing is the depreciation. A new mobile home will lose about 25 percent of its total value when it leaves the sales lot. Consider purchasing a previously owned mobile home, because someone else has already taken the depreciation.

PURCHASE OPTIONS

Now that you've decided what type of house you want to buy, you need to decide how to pay for it. In order to serve God in the very best way, the goal of all Christians should be to become debt-free—and that includes their house. If you choose to borrow money to purchase the house, you should make it your goal to pay the house off as soon as possible. Several ways to do this will be discussed later in this booklet.

PAY CASH

The best way to buy a house is to pay cash if you are financially able. The idea of owning a house debt-free is not a new one; in fact, it's quite ancient. Most families used to own their houses, and those who didn't were abnormal. Those who couldn't afford the large house they wanted simply bought a smaller house, put a great deal of time and effort into it, improved its value, sold it, and bought the next sized house. Eventually they got their dream house without going into debt. (See examples of the Bigs versus the Smalls below.)

INSTITUTIONAL LOANS

If you have to borrow to buy your house, an institutional loan (from a bank, savings and loan, credit union, or mortgage company) is perhaps the most common type of loan, although it may not necessarily be the best type for you. It's very important to shop around with this type of loan because there are so many variables. As you enter the marketplace of house buyers, you should know what type of loans are available to you and what additional costs are associated with each.

FEES AND CONTRACTS

Most institutional loans require a down payment—usually 5 to 20 percent, but you should put more down if possible—and various "closing costs." Closing costs can include loan origination fees, points, attorney's fees, survey fees, appraisal fees, PMI (private mortgage insurance), real estate commissions, credit reports, title search fees, and more. These fees can add up to a significant expense—several thousand dollars— and should be researched thoroughly when considering any loan. Many times the seller may pay for some or all of the closing costs.

If your offer to purchase the house is subject to selling your present house, getting financial approval, or waiting on results from various inspections, including radon gas testing, termite inspections, appliance and structural inspections, or water testing, make sure these contingencies are spelled out in the contract.

Housing

FIXED-RATE MORTGAGES

This is an excellent form of home loan. You know exactly what the interest rate and monthly mortgage payment will be and whether it will fit into your budget. Although a fixed-rate loan will have slightly higher interest rates than other types of loans, it will not change during the life of the loan. You know what the terms will be for the next fifteen or thirty years. Shop around for the lowest interest rate, since they do vary from institution to institution and from week to week.

ADJUSTABLE RATE MORTGAGES (ARMS)

Adjustable rate mortgages are not a bad form of home loan, provided you can get an interest rate lower than the prevailing fixed rate and the loan contains a cap on the maximum increase during the life of the loan. These loans fluctuate with the economy; therefore it's important to know exactly how high the interest rate could go. Most ARMs begin with an interest rate that's a percentage point or two below current fixed-rate loans and are "adjusted" every year after that. This makes it possible for more couples to "qualify" for these loans but makes it hard to establish exactly how much to budget for housing expenses from year to year.

Make sure you understand the terms before you choose this type of loan. For example, if you can get an 11 percent ARM with a 5 percent cap —or a maximum rate of 16 percent— and the current fixed rate is 13 percent, you would be better off to accept the ARM than the fixed-rate mortgage. However, you need to figure out what your monthly payment would be if the interest rate rose to 16 percent. Would that payment fit into your budget comfortably?

One last point to consider on adjustable rate loans is the duration of the loan. Many of these loans are short-term loans and can be renewed at the lender's option. Stay away from these short-term loans unless you know you can pay off the house in that amount of time. There is no guarantee you'll be able to renegotiate another loan you can afford, and you could lose your house.

"PAYDAY" MORTGAGES

"Pay-day" mortgages are designed to increase the frequency of your loan payments. Instead of paying a monthly payment, the house buyer pays one-half of the monthly payment every other week. Since more of the payment is applied to the principal, equity is accrued at a faster rate. This will consequently reduce the life of the loan, and the borrower reaps the benefits of paying less interest and paying off the house mortgage early. Some lenders don't offer this type of loan because they lose interest. However, this financing option is being offered by more and more lenders due to increasing competition for loans.

The following chart compares different payments of a $60,000 mortgage at 12 percent.

$60,000 Mortgage at 12 Percent

	P/I	Life of Loan (years)	Interest Paid	Interest Saved
Weekly	$154.29	18.79	$90,809.33	$71,372.20
Biweekly	$308.59	19.04	$92,752.05	$69,429.15
Conventional	$617.17	30	$162,181.20	-0-

ASSUMABLE MORTGAGE

This is an existing mortgage that the buyer assumes at the existing terms of the seller's loan. Assumable mortgages benefit the buyer because the interest rate and mortgage payment are usually lower than current rates. Check to see if there is an assumption fee and if the loan will be assumable if you sell the house to someone else.

GOVERNMENT FINANCING

Purchasing a house with a loan subsidized by the government may be a matter of concern to some people. Although no biblical principles specifically apply to this subject, it is my personal opinion that Christians should look not to the government for help but rather to God. By depending on the government to supply more and more of our basic needs, we run the risk of eventually losing our trust in God. If you have prayed about it and still think you should take advantage of the subsidized loan, then by all means follow the conscience the Lord gave you.

There are several types of government loans that may be obtained through your local banking institution. VA, FHA, and state-bonded programs are attractive to house buyers because of the low interest rates and the low down payment required. Be careful not to get yourself into surety with these types of loans.

SELLER FINANCING

The seller may finance the house through a land sales contract or trust deed for the buyer. This provides a steady income to the seller, and the buyer usually gets the financing for a percent or two lower than current interest rates and saves on closing costs. Be sure a qualified attorney draws up all legal papers so there is no question about the terms of the sale.

EQUITY SHARING

This is an excellent way for a couple to get help in purchasing a home and for an investor to receive a healthy return on a relatively small investment. This is the way it works. A couple needing help in obtaining funds for a down payment on a mortgage locates an investor willing to provide a certain portion of those funds. A written agreement is drawn up that defines the number of years the house will be retained by the buyer and the amount of equity that will be paid to the investor once the house is sold. Usually the investor will receive his full investment back plus 50 percent of any profit.

A provision should be made so that if the couple wants to keep their home after a period of years, the investor will be repaid with a predetermined amount of interest on his original loan. In order to avoid any differences, a good Christian attorney should be involved in the preparation of any equity-sharing plan.

PARENT-ASSISTED FINANCING

I believe it is the parents' responsibility to help their children reasonably—but not to carry all their burdens. One way to help them is by joint ownership. For example, a parent puts up the down payment for his son or daughter to buy a house, and the home is in joint ownership, so the parent owns a part of it and the child owns a part of it. The parent then rents the house back to the child. The parent receives the income, depreciates the house, and takes it off his taxes, while the child rents it, retains partial ownership, and profits from the eventual sale. The child should care for repairs and maintenance. This method benefits both parents and child and may also be used by Christians willing to help young Christian couples get into their first house.

Parents with substantial savings may also choose to be the lender for their children. This method will save money on closing costs and can be a source of retirement income for the parents. Make sure, however, that the children are mature enough to be responsible for this generosity and that they do not take advantage of the parents. All legal forms should be drawn up and on record so there are no questions if the parents or the children pass away or in the event of default. Parental financing should be viewed by both parties with the same financial commitment and consequences as any other type of financing.

SELLING YOUR HOUSE

If you are on the other side of the coin and are selling a house, there are certain things you should know. First, you must decide who is going to sell your house.

BY OWNER

You can elect to sell your house yourself in order to save the cost of a real estate agent's commission. This means you advertise it yourself and must be available to show the house to interested buyers. Be knowledgeable about selling your house. Know what other houses in your area are selling for, and understand what you must do when someone contracts to buy the house. Have a qualified attorney review all offers before you sign anything.

BY REAL ESTATE AGENTS

You may choose to have an agent sell the house for you. This will give you greater exposure in the real estate market. It may save you time and money because the agent can advertise, use the Multiple Listing Service, and show the house while you are at work. You will have to pay the agent's commission—about 5 to 10 percent of the selling price—if your house sells. Have the broker explain every offer that is made for the purchase of your home. You may choose to have an attorney review all offers if you are not knowledgeable in real estate.

OTHER CONSIDERATIONS WHEN SELLING YOUR HOME

TAX CONSEQUENCES

If you sell your house and buy

another that costs less than the house you sold, you must pay a capital gains tax on the difference between the two houses. However, there are allowances for selling costs and improvements that can reduce the gain. You may postpone tax payment if you buy a more expensive house within two years. There is also a one-time exclusion on capital gains for anyone more than fifty-five years old. You may want to contact a professional CPA or tax adviser for additional help.

CONTINUED LIABILITY

You can be held liable for any loan a buyer assumes from you if the buyer defaults, unless you obtain a total release from liability. Contact the lending institution for more information about obtaining one of these releases. Check to see if there is a fee involved.

EARNEST MONEY CONTRACTS

When someone is genuinely interested in buying your house, he or she will submit a contract and earnest money. This is a deposit on the house so that you won't sell it to anyone else while the potential buyer is getting financing approved, selling his house, or awaiting inspection results. At this time you should be willing to explain any problems or situations to the buyer about the house. Not only will it save the buyer some headaches down the road, but you will be setting a wonderful Christian example. This is also the time to declare which items will be included in the purchase price. Some items to consider are appliances, curtains, swing sets, firewood, or maintenance equipment. You may desire to present a counteroffer, showing any terms of their offer you are unwilling to accept.

QUESTIONS ABOUT REFINANCING

Should I refinance to obtain a lower interest rate? If you are considering refinancing your house to take advantage of lower interest rates, determine if it will actually save you money by figuring the dollar amount of interest you will save compared to the costs of refinancing. Some banks will require new title searches, surveys, and appraisals to refinance your loan. Local court recording fees of the mortgage itself will usually be necessary, and there are often points to be paid for a new loan. If you can easily reclaim these expenses through the savings in interest within a few years, refinancing is for you. You will usually benefit through refinancing if the new interest rate is 3 percent lower than your present mortgage.

Should I get a home equity loan (second mortgage) to pay off my consumer debts? Proverbs 3:27-28 says, "Do not withhold good from those to whom it is due. . . . Do not say to your neighbor, 'Go and come back, and tomorrow I will give it,' when you have it with you." If you can't pay your bills on a regular basis and you have the means to pay those bills, God requires that you do whatever it takes to pay them off. Unfortunately, borrowing more money, especially against the equity in your home, usually doesn't solve the problem. It only treats a symptom. You must treat the problem itself. If you are having problems with your credit cards, cut them up. Establish a budgeted payment plan, and repay each creditor. Work at paying off the smallest debt first, then the next, and so on. Remember, the borrower becomes the lender's slave.

Should I use a home equity loan to free cash to invest? If you are thinking about borrowing the equity from your house for other investments, remember that Proverbs 14:15 says, "The naive believes everything, but the prudent man considers his steps." Some of the worst advice ever given was to suggest that anyone borrow from the equity in his or her house to invest somewhere else. Ask yourself this question: Do you and your spouse consider your house to be "just another investment"? How would your spouse and family be affected if you lost your house because the "investment" went bad? There is always some degree of risk in any investment, and the money can be lost, but the mortgage on the house will still be there. All Christians should aim to own their house debt-free. Our generation believes we can never own a house debt-free; therefore, we treat it as an investment. With rare exceptions, a house is not an investment; it is a purchase. If you want to invest, save your money. Use your house for what it was intended—the comfort and welfare of your family.

OTHER QUESTIONS
ABOUT REAL ESTATE

What happens if the bank forecloses on my house? Although foreclosure is a serious problem, it does not mean God has washed His hands of you. Losing your house will teach you a costly, yet valuable, lesson on the danger of surety. And although you may not be held legally responsible for the difference between the amount of your mortgage and the price the lender receives from the sale of the house, morally you are responsible for this debt. When you enter into a contract, you are bound by your word to fulfill its intent. (Remember Psalm 37:21.) Once the foreclosure has been finalized, work out a payment plan that will fit into your adjusted budget for the balance.

The lender will always have the option to file a deficiency judgment against you. He may retain this right for several years. Check your state laws. He may choose to release you from the deficiency debt. He is the master and has this right. You must commit to pay the deficiency and do whatever the lender requests.

If you are fortunate enough to deed the home to the lender instead of being foreclosed on, you may avoid paying anything, but you will still lose the house and equity. If you have fallen behind on your payments or must move quickly, make every effort to sell your house even if you have to take a loss. Since foreclosed houses are generally sold at auction for much less than fair market value, you can often sell it for more, thus reducing the amount you must pay back.

What type of insurance should I have on my house? Most lending institutions require that you have enough insurance to cover the amount of the mortgage. A home owner's insurance policy is a comprehensive insurance plan covering the home, its contents, and any liability associated with the property. Usually a home owner's policy is the least expensive way to insure a dwelling. You can get a fire policy only, but it isn't as comprehensive as a home owner's policy. Shop around before you buy any insurance because there can be a significant difference in the cost of insurance from one company to another.

If you buy a condominium or mobile home, most insurance companies provide specialized insurance for these types of dwellings. (For more information on insurance, see booklet titled *Insurance Plans* in this series.)

Should I have life insurance to cover my house? It is wise for a family to have life insurance to pay their house off. This insurance is commonly called mortgage life insurance.

Mortgage life insurance is usually sold through the lender where you received your house loan, but this can be an expensive way to purchase life insurance. A decreasing term insurance policy through your local insurance agent may be less expensive.

The best option would be to determine what your total life insurance needs are and include your house loan balance with this. Purchasing one policy instead of having several different life insurance policies will save you money. As your need for death protection diminishes, you can reduce your coverage.

What type of prepayment options are available? After you have made your regular monthly payment, any additional funds you put toward your mortgage go directly to the principal, exclusive of any interest. Therefore, the next month you're paying slightly less interest and slightly more principal on the unpaid balance. Each month you prepay part of the principal, a greater amount goes toward the principal the following month, since your regular payment amount stays constant. According to this prepayment method, a $60,000 mortgage at 10 percent for 30 years can be reduced by approximately $68,500 and 16 years by prepaying an additional $100 per month. You may want to write two separate checks, one for the regular monthly payment and one for the additional principal —write "principal" on this check, to make sure there is no confusion at the lending institution.

$60,000 Mortgage at 10 Percent

	P/I	Life of Loan (years)	Interest Paid	Interest Saved
Conventional	$526	30	$129,360	-0-
Additional $25	$551	23.8	$97,586	$31,774
Additional $50	$576	20	$78,240	$51,120
Additional $100	$626	16	$60,818	$68,542

The "payday" mortgage is another prepayment option. See the paragraph under "Institutional Loans" above.

Before making any prepayments on your mortgage, check with your lending institution about any penalties, and request an annual amortization schedule to monitor the reduction in your principal balance.

Many families will be able to make extra monthly principal payments—of $50 or $100—and pay their loans off earlier than scheduled. This may be the simplest option for most families.

The following examples of the Bigs versus the Smalls are primarily to show the future value of money over time and the tremendous cost of borrowing money.

Case Study 1:

Facts: Bill Big and Sam Small were fraternity brothers. Both are now married and want to buy homes in the same subdivision. Both have $10,000 for a cash down payment. Both families have $28,000 incomes, and the mortgage company has approved both for monthly house payments of $535. Their dream houses cost $70,000 each. Assume no inflation and no appreciation in real estate.

THE BIGS

$70,000	Cost
-10,000	Cash Down Payment
$60,000	Mortgage – 30 Years
	10 % Interest Rate,
	$527 Monthly Payment

$189,720   Total cash expended after 30 years

Housing

The Smalls sold their house at the end of 7 years for $40,000 cash and bought their dream house next door to the Bigs.

THE SMALLS

$40,000	Cost – Bought a smaller house
- 8,000	Cash Down Payment
$32,000	Mortgage – 7 Years
	10% Interest Rate,
	$531 Monthly Payment
$70,000	Cost
-40,000	Cash Down Payment
$30,000	Mortgage – 7 Years
	10% Interest Rate,
	$498 Monthly Payment

House is paid off after 14 years:

$44,604	(7 years at $531/Month)
+41,832	(7 years at $498/Month)
$86,436	Total cost of house

$86,436	Cost of House
+95,616	Invested $498/Month into a money market account for 16 uears, after paying the mortgage.
$182,052	Total cash expended for 30 years
$192,830	Value of money market account after 16 years at 8% interest.

Case Study 2

Dream house: $70,000; Income: $28,000; Approved monthly payments: $535

THE BIGS

$70,000 Cost
-10,000   Cash Down Payment
$60,000 Mortgage – 30 Years
          10 % Interest Rate,
          $527 Monthly Payment

$189,720 – Total cash expended after 30 years

Housing

THE SMALLS

$60,000	Cost – Bought a smaller house
-10,000	Cash Down Payment
$50,000	Mortgage – 30 Years,
	10% Interest Rate,
	$439 Monthly Payment

The Smalls decided to pay an additional payment on the principal of
$100 per month.

| $100 | Principal Payment |
| $539 | Total Monthly Payment |

House is paid off in just under 15 years.

$96,481	Cost of House
+97,020	Invested $539/Month into a money market account for 15 years.
$193,501	Total cash expended for 30 years.
$186,514	Value of money market account after 16 years at 8% interest, assuming taxes are deferred.

49

Is buying foreclosed homes ethical? Are we disobeying what God's Word says about robbing the poor when we buy foreclosed homes? A Christian first must ask himself, "Did I help to cause the problems that generated the foreclosure?" In other words, did you lend somebody money he or she could not pay back and then foreclose on the home? If so, you would be guilty of robbing the poor.

The second question that a Christian has to ask is, "Am I being fair?" Have you willfully taken advantage of someone else's misery? In practical fact, these people are going to lose their houses regardless of whether you buy them out of foreclosure because the bank is going to foreclose. As long as you did not generate the foreclosure, there is nothing scripturally wrong with buying a foreclosed house. If you can get to the family before they get into foreclosure, you could save them some money they might lose otherwise. Remember what Paul wrote in Philippians 2:3, "Do nothing from selfishness or empty conceit, but with humility of mind let each of you regard one another as more important than himself."

Am I too old to buy a house? One of the foundational blocks of a biblically-oriented financial plan is a debt-free home. This should be the goal of all Christians but particularly so for retirees. Anything can happen to the economy. It may be a depression brought on by a financial collapse or hyperinflation brought on by printing massive amounts of money to avoid a depression. Either way, you can lose whatever is indebted. A debt-free home is yours, not the lender's.

Personally, I would do whatever is necessary to become debt-free at age sixty-five or older. If it were necessary to sell a larger house and pare down expenses by buying a smaller, debt-free house, I would do that. We are a nation of debtors, and eventually we will grasp the meaning of Proverbs 22:7, "The rich rules over the poor, and the borrower becomes the lender's slave." (For more ways to avoid debt see *Financial Freedom*.)

To a great extent your circumstances will determine whether or not you should buy a house. Don't put yourself in jeopardy just to "own" a house. If you have a "certain" way to pay for the house, it may be a good idea. However, if you are older, don't depend on your health or your job to make mortgage payments. Both can easily be lost.

Should I pay off my mortgage and lose the tax deduction? People who borrow to purchase houses often believe that the tax breaks they receive justify the interest that is paid. Those who are in the 28-percent tax bracket and pay $1,000 in interest in a year may receive a $280 tax credit. Obviously that $720 went into someone else's pocket—the lender's. Refer to the illustration of the Bigs and Smalls to see that the best alternative is to pay off your home mortgage as early as possible and not only save the interest but accumulate a sizable savings as well. That far outweighs any tax deductions you may receive from paying interest.

TIPS ON HOUSING EXPENDITURES

Typically, this is one of the largest home budget problems. Many families buy a home they can't afford, motivated by peer or some other pressure. It is not necessary for everyone to own a home. The decision to buy or rent should be based on needs and financial ability rather than internal or external pressure.

The following are some hints to observe:

1. Purchase a home only if the total payments (mortgage, taxes, insurance, and so on) do not exceed 40 percent of your net income.
2. Do not finance a second mortgage for the down payment.
3. Consider the monthly upkeep of a home. This usually averages 10 percent of the monthly payment.
4. Consider the tax deduction for interest paid as a reduction in monthly payment.
5. If trading, consider whether you need to do so.
6. Secure at least three estimates for insurance. Normally insurance needs can best be satisfied with a comprehensive package (home owner's, renter's policy, and so on). Use of the deductible feature will substantially reduce premiums.

Buying a Car

The advertising media refer to us as "consumers," but that's not always the best description. I believe P. T. Barnum had a more apt word—*suckers*. Often we are unwise in our decision-making when it comes to our machines—especially our cars.

Many families buy new cars they cannot afford and trade them long before their utility is depleted. Those who buy a new car, keep it for less than four years, and then trade it for a new model waste the maximum amount of money. Some people such as salesmen who drive a great deal need new cars frequently, but most of us do not. We trade cars because we want to, not because we have to. Many factors come into play here, such as ego, esteem, maturity, and so on. But few Christians seek God's will when they purchase cars, so they suffer later because of the financial strains they place on their finances.

In our society owning a car is a fact of life. To be sure, some people, particularly in large urban areas, are able to get about using public transportation, but the lifestyle of today's average family makes owning at least one car a practical necessity. So with the need for a car a given, what is the most economical way to obtain it?

PRELIMINARY STEPS

EXAMINE YOUR MOTIVES

Let's face it. The majority of new automobile sales in the U.S. are made because of the buyer's wants, not his needs. In fact, a significant portion of people who are shopping for cars— new or used—simply do not need them. Often they are just tired of their car; it looks old and out-of-date, or it needs major repairs to put it back into top condition, or their neighbors or co-workers have acquired new cars. We have been programmed to think that if any of these conditions exists, we are justified in acquiring another— preferably new—car.

Cars do wear out, and everyone eventually finds himself or herself in the position of having to get another car. We all, however, would do well to examine our motives first. Often the notion to buy a car springs from the emotional rather than the rational side of our nature.

DETERMINE YOUR NEEDS

Having examined your motives, the next step is to determine your needs. Luke 14:28 says, "For which one of you, when he wants to build a tower, does not first sit down and calculate the cost, to see if he has enough to complete it?" Most everyone would naturally like to be sitting behind the wheel of a shiny new automobile. But have they calculated the cost? They need to consider not only whether they can afford it but also whether buying a new car is the best stewardship of their family's hard-earned money.

Costs (payments, insurance, maintenance, and so on) for a mid-range new car commonly run in excess of $300 a month. That kind of extra expense can wreck the average family's budget. Sure, they may be able to make the monthly payments, but the other budget categories such as food and clothes will suffer, and since those are major needs, the family will inevitably go into debt to obtain them.

The average family needs to buy a good quality, reliable, used car. Of course the size, style, age, and appearance of the car will vary from family to family.

BECOME AN INFORMED BUYER

Doing your homework before you begin shopping for a car can help you find the car that is best suited to your needs. Consumer advocacy groups and publications such as *Consumer Report* provide information on the safety, maintenance, and value of various car models. Remember too that cheaper does not always mean better.

Friends and family members are also a good source of information. Talk with owners of cars similar to the model you are considering to see if they are satisfied.

SHOPPING FOR A USED CAR

FRIENDS

Once you have determined the type of car you want and can afford, the next step is to find the car. Go to your closest friends first. Let them

know you're looking for a car. Find
out if there is a Christian family in
your church with a car to sell that
will fit your needs. Before most
Christians will sell their car to somebody they know, they will either tell
him everything that is wrong with
the car or else have it fixed. By purchasing directly from the owner, you
can learn the history of the car and
usually negotiate the best possible
price.

LEASING COMPANIES

A second good source of used
cars is a leasing company. Many of
these companies keep their cars one
or two years and then resell them.
Most of these cars have been routine-
ly maintained, have low "highway"
mileage, and are available for a fair
price. Often a car obtained from a
leasing company will come with a
one-year warranty.

BANKS

A third good source is your local
banker. Let him know that if he gets
a really good car as a repossession
(where the bank has to recover the
car), you are interested in buying it.
Be aware that a repossessed car prob-

ably will need some repairs since its owner most likely couldn't afford to keep it maintained properly. Make sure that you have some money in reserve for this purpose.

CAR DEALERS

Dealers have the largest selection of used cars available. A used car that was locally owned can be a good deal, especially if you are able to contact the previous owner to see if there are any hidden problems with the car.

ADVERTISEMENTS

A fourth source is advertisements through newspapers and similar publications. The difficulty in using this source is that you don't know the seller, and the seller doesn't know you. Unfortunately, there are a lot of unethical, dishonest people out there with cars for sale.

Before buying any used car, it is advisable to write out an affidavit that says, "I swear that the car that I am selling, to my knowledge, has no obvious defects, has no rust that I know about, and that the mileage on the odometer is correct and accurate." Have the seller sign it (before a notary if possible). Most honest people won't object, and most dishonest ones won't sign it.

Finally, have a mechanic check the car for defects or problems that may not be obvious to you, such as hidden rust, signs of having been in an accident, and engine problems. The dollars you spend having a mechanic look at the car can save you much grief and expense later.

PAYING FOR THE CAR

The best way to finance a car is not to finance it at all. It is always the best policy to save the money and pay cash for your car. Auto financing is poor stewardship at best. But assuming that for some reason or another an individual thinks he or she must finance the purchase of the car, some basic guidelines should be followed:

1. Do not finance through the car dealership if at all possible. Arranging for a loan through a bank or other financial institution instead can allow you to negotiate with the dealer on a "cash basis." When you do arrange a loan, be sure it is a simple interest loan with no pay-off restrictions. If you do that, at least you have the capability to become debt-free within a short period of time.

2. *Do not trade in your old car—sell it*. If a car dealer can sell your car and make a profit, so can you. It certainly takes more time and effort to sell your car, but it is worth it. Advertise your car by a notice in the newspaper or a sign in the window. Provided your car is in reasonable shape, it shouldn't take very long to sell.

3. *If your old car is not paid off, keep it until it is*. If you trade in a car with a mortgage on it, you are simply taking your current debt and refinancing it into a new car, effectively doubling the interest you have been paying on your old mortgage.

QUESTIONS ABOUT BUYING A CAR

Should I buy an extended warranty on my new car? If you are considering an extended warranty, you need to ask several questions. First, does the warranty cover a period of time or a number of miles not covered under any other implied warranties? Second, does the extended warranty cover parts and labor, or parts only? Third, does the price of the extended warranty seem reasonable in relation to the price of the parts covered?

If an extended warranty covers five years or 50,000 miles, the average driver will really only get coverage for approximately three years since the average person drives more than 10,000 miles per year. A better warranty would cover five years or 100,000 miles.

If only parts are covered, the cost of labor is usually so great that the owner will not get the full benefit of the extended warranty unless each part covered is more expensive than the relative cost of the warranty.

How much of our family budget should be designated for car expenses? About 15 to 17 percent of your net spendable income (after deducting tithes and taxes) should be allotted for automobile expenses. That includes payments, gasoline, oil, maintenance, and insurance.

What are some ways I can cut my car expenses? First, you can save money on car insurance. The average family's car is more than three years old. The only kind of insurance to have on that car is liability, which is required by law. Shop and compare prices on liability insurance.

Second, you can save money on tires. Go to a tire dealer, and ask if he sells "take-offs," which are tires that have been taken off a new car because the buyer wanted a different kind. Take-offs are nearly new and may be half the price of brand-new tires.

Third, consider starting a car maintenance co-op, or join an existing one. A typical co-op involves a group of Christians who meet regularly at a church parking lot to perform routine maintenance and car repairs for one another.

Preventive maintenance will save on towing charges due to unexpected breakdowns on the highway. Check your local library for books on car ownership that offer other money-saving tips.

What about leasing a car? Leasing a car often seems attractive to those who cannot otherwise afford a new car because it involves little or no down payment. However, that means that the whole cost of a leased vehicle is financed for the entire lease period. Also, the lease is a contract to pay that is just as binding as a purchase contract and places the lessee in a position of surety.

For example, if the lessee runs into unexpected financial problems, he cannot sell the car outright because he does not hold the title (the leasing company does). Even if the leasing company would arrange for the sale of the car (and it is under no obligation to do so), the amount owed on the lease is almost always more than the car is worth, leaving the lessee with no car and still owing more money!

Again, what is surety? The book of Proverbs has more than twenty references to the principle of surety. Remember that "surety" is taking on an obligation to pay something without an absolutely certain way to pay it. Proverbs 22:26 says, "Do not be among those who give pledges, among those who become sureties for debts."

To keep from becoming surety, the best policy is never to borrow. But if you do borrow, make sure that the item for which you borrowed is total collateral and that you would not be liable for any deficiency beyond that.

BUDGET HINTS FOR AUTO OWNERS

Can your present car be repaired

without great expense? How many miles are left on it?

Does your budget allow for a new car?

Do you really need a brand-new car, or will a used one do? (Unless the purchase is for business use, the new car may be unnecessary.)

Bargain for a short-term 100 percent guarantee on a used car. (Avoid any percentage contract—you will lose.)

Do not be pressured by sales tactics. Set your own price and the type of car you desire, and be willing to lose the "good deals" that require quick decisions.

Be willing to accept minor difficulties on a used car to secure substantial price reductions. (Be sure you anticipate those repairs.)

If buying a new car, avoid purchasing a new model when it first comes out. (Buy year-end close-outs or demonstrators.)

A cheaper model with the same options as the luxury model will provide substantial savings (just a little less prestige).

Avoid the use of credit life insurance. It is expensive and unnecessary if you have an adequate insurance program.

Secure estimates from at least three major insurance companies before purchasing. Use at least $100 deductibles. As stated in a previous section, evaluate as follows:

1. Select adequate liability coverage.
2. Consider collision and comprehensive coverage. Note: It is important to determine whether you can afford to have your car repaired if you have an accident where you are at fault.
3. Do you need medical benefits?

MAINTAINING CARS

Learn to perform routine maintenance: oil change, lubrication, tune-up, and so on. The purchase of approximately $25 worth of tools will return at least $100 per year in service costs and repair bills.

Repair minor conditions yourself, and do them immediately. Do not let "little" problems pile up, or you will be tempted to trade in your car.

Purchase oil, grease, spark plugs, and points from a wholesale distributor. Use the best grades only, and try to combine purchases with two or more friends for best buys.

Use a written maintenance chart for every car, and attend to routine maintenance diligently. Regular maintenance will extend the life of a car.

Look into purchasing "take-off" tires from dealers who service fleet cars and cars owned by government agencies. First-line radial tires that provide more mileage than most second-line new tires are available.

Check your car's gasoline rating, and use the cheapest gasoline recommended.

Conclusions

Honestly evaluate your need for a car. If you determine your need justifies a purchase, buy a used car. Shop for value, not just the lowest price. Save for your car and pay cash. However, if you must borrow, go through an institution other than the dealership. Arrange for a simple interest loan with no pay-off restrictions. Then negotiate with the dealer on a cash basis. Finally, rather than trading your old car, sell it.

Appliances and Furniture

Though not as expensive as housing or automobiles, other household items such as appliances and furniture are often purchased on credit. They can also consume a high portion of the family budget.

PURCHASING APPLIANCES

Use a consumer buying guide to determine the best manufacturer.

Select a unit based on its functional use, not its dials and gadgets. (Deluxe models cost more but do not perform better and usually require more maintenance.)

Shop around and compare prices on the leading products. Keep a written record of your findings.

Look for volume dealers who carry name-brand products under their own labels.

Purchase the item on a cash basis without a trade-in (the seller will discount for cash without trade).

Avoid dealer service contracts. They are sometimes expensive and often frustrating. (If the product warranty is not sufficient, look for another brand.)

Insist on free delivery and installation. (Dealer may resist initially but will probably agree.)

Look for similar used units in the paper or shopper's guide.

REDUCING HOUSEHOLD APPLIANCE COSTS

Review service manuals for ordinary maintenance care, and perform as often as required.

Keep a written maintenance chart on or near the unit.

Purchase a shop manual from manufacturer. (Most major manufacturers will sell this upon written request.)

Use the unit within suggested standards. (Example: do not overload washers and dryers.)

If a unit out of warranty breaks down, use the fix-it guide to determine the problem and repair if possible. Before calling outside service, seek free counsel from Christian friends (often someone you know is a fix-it type).

Before discarding the old unit for a new one, consider an overhaul of the existing machine.

REDUCING FURNITURE COSTS

Consult a consumer buying index for best purchase value.

Consider repairing and rebuilding used furniture of good quality. (Many good fix-it guides explain how to refinish and reupholster furniture.)

Consult local shopper's guide for good quality buys.

Shop local garage sales.

Shop for discontinued furniture lines.

HOME FINANCES AND HOW THEY RELATE TO MAJOR PURCHASES

All financial decisions regarding major purchases must be made within the context of a well-defined family budget plan.

The following is a summarized list of the financial principles applicable to home financial planning. Study these and apply them. Then share God's blessings with others around you.

I. Principles of home finances
   A. Use a written plan
   B. Provide for the Lord's work first
   C. Excel at your tasks
   D. Limit credit
   E. Think before buying
      1. Is it necessary?
      2. Does it reflect your Christian ethic?
      3. Is it the best buy?
      4. Is it an impulse item?
      5. Does it add to or detract from the family?
      6. Is it a highly depreciable item?
      7. Does it require costly upkeep?

F. Practice saving money regularly
G. Set your own goals—with your family
H. Get out of debt
I. Limit business involvement
J. Avoid indulgences, lavishness
K. Seek good Christian counsel
L. Stick to your plans

II. Purpose of a budget
   A. To define income versus expense
   B. To detect problem areas
   C. To provide a written plan
   D. To aid in follow-up
   E. To schedule money in and out of the home

III. What a budget will do
   A. Help you visualize your goals
   B. Provide a written point of reference for husband and wife
   C. Help family communications
   D. Provide a written reminder
   E. Reflect your habits

IV. What a budget will not do
   A. Solve your immediate problems
   B. Make you use it
   C. Take the place of action

V. How to
  A. Calculate actual expenses
    1. Use a thirty-day expense diary or notebook
    2. Use a checking account ledger
    3. Use a creditor ledger showing each debt due
  B. Make out a family budget
    1. Define actual expenditures (present budget)
    2. Define proposed expenditures (future budget)
    3. Calculate income
    4. Calculate fixed expenses
    5. Calculate variable expenses
  C. Use a budget
    1. Post it in the open
    2. Set an achievable goal
    3. Keep it up to date
    4. Establish a set time and day to review it

A workbook series on Christian finances is also available for those who would like to study or teach these principles. Contact your local Christian bookstore, and ask for *How to Manage Your Money*.

Housing, automobile, and other major goods play a major role in your overall family budget. On the

following page, calculate how these
items figure into your total budget
and what adjustments you should
make in each area to achieve a balance.

Major Purchases

The Family Budget Guide
(Monthly Income and Expenses)

INCOME PER MONTH   _____
  Salary   _____
  Interest   _____
  Dividends   _____
  Notes   _____
  Rents   _____
  TOTAL GROSS INCOME   _____

Less:
1. Tithe   _____
2. Tax   _____
NET SPENDABLE INCOME   _____
3. Housing 38%*
      Mortgage (rent)   _____
      Insurance   _____
      Taxes   _____
      Electricity   _____
      Gas   _____
      Water   _____
      Sanitation   _____
      Telephone   _____
      Maintenance   _____
      Other   _____
4. Food 12%   _____
5. Automobile(s) 15%   _____
      Payments   _____
      Gas and Oil   _____
      Insurance   _____
      License   _____
      Taxes   _____
      Maintenance/Repair/
        Replacement   _____
6. Insurance 5%   _____
      Life   _____
      Medical   _____
      Other   _____
7. Debts 5%   _____
      Credit Card   _____
      Loans and Notes   _____
      Other   _____

* Percentages based on a $25,000 gross annual income.

Appliances and Furniture

8. Entertainment and
   Recreation 5%   _____
9. Clothing 5%   _____
10. Savings 5%   _____
11. Medical Expenses 5%   _____
    Doctor   _____
12. Miscellaneous 5%   _____
    Toiletry, Cosmetics   _____
    Beauty, Barber   _____
    Laundry, Cleaning   _____
    Allowances, Lunches   _____
    Subscriptions   _____
    Gifts (incl. Christmas)   _____
    Special education   _____
    Cash   _____
    Other   _____
13. School/Child Care 10%   _____
    (If you use this budget cate-
    gory, the percentages of the
    other categories must be re-
    duced by an equal amount.)
    TOTAL EXPENSES   _____

INCOME VERSUS EXPENSE
  Net Spendable Income   _____
  Less Expenses   _____
  Total (Deficit/Surplus)   _____

Other Materials by Larry Burkett:

Books in this series:

Financial Freedom
Sound Investments
Major Purchases
Insurance Plans
Giving and Tithing
Personal Finances

Other Books:

Debt-Free Living
Financial Planning Workbook
How to Manage Your Money
Your Finances in Changing Times

Videos:

Your Finances in Changing Times
Two Masters
How to Manage Your Money
The Financial Planning Workbook

Other Resources:

Financial Planning Organizer
Debt-Free Living Cassette